D1588397

POSITIVELY
POOH

A Book of
Happy Thoughts

EGMONT

We bring stories to life

First published in Great Britain 2005 by Egmont UK Limited
239 Kensington High Street, London W8 6SA

Selected text from *WINNIE-THE-POOH* and *THE HOUSE AT POOH CORNER* by A. A. Milne
© The Trustees of the Pooh Properties

Line drawings © E.H. Shepard, colouring © 1970, 1973 and 1974 E.H. Shepard and Egmont UK Ltd

Sketches from THE POOH SKETCHBOOK copyright © 1982 Lloyds TSB Bank PLC
Executors of the Estate of E.H. Shepard, and the E.H. Shepard Trust

This edition © 2006 The Trustees of the Pooh Properties

Book design and new text © 2006 Egmont UK Ltd

ISBN 978 1 4052 2049 1
ISBN 1 4052 2049 X

3 5 7 9 10 8 6 4 2

A CIP catalogue record for this title is available from the British Library

Printed and bound in Malaysia

POSITIVELY POOH

A Book of Happy Thoughts

A.A. Milne

Illustrated by E.H. Shepard

EGMONT

Know you are important in
lots of ways to lots of people

And then this Bear, Pooh Bear, Winnie-the-Pooh, F.O.P. (Friend of Piglet's), R.C. (Rabbit's Companion), P.D. (Pole Discoverer), E.C. and T.F. (Eeyore's Comforter and Tail-finder) – in fact, Pooh himself . . .

And the door opened, and Owl looked out.
'Hallo, Pooh,' he said. 'How's things?'
'Terrible and Sad,' said Pooh, 'because Eeyore,
who is a friend of mine, has lost his tail.
And he's Moping about it. So could you very
kindly tell me how to find it for him?'

You are not alone

There's a funny side
to everything

'Whatever's the matter, Piglet?' said Christopher
Robin, who was just getting up.
'Heff,' said Piglet, breathing so hard that he could
hardly speak, 'A Heff – a Heff – a Heffalump.'
'Where?'
'Up there,' said Piglet, waving his paw.
'What did it look like?'

'It had the biggest head you ever saw, Christopher
Robin. A great enormous thing, like – like nothing . . . I
don't know – like an enormous big nothing. Like a jar.'
  'Well,' said Christopher Robin, putting on his shoes,
        'I shall go and look at it. Come on.'
    Piglet wasn't afraid if he had Christopher Robin
          with him, so off they went . . .
      'I can hear it, can't you?' said Piglet anxiously,
              as they got near.
      'I can hear *something*,' said Christopher Robin.
        It was Pooh bumping his head against a
                tree-root he had found.
    'There!' said Piglet. 'Isn't it *awful*?' And he held
        on tight to Christopher Robin's hand.
  Suddenly Christopher Robin began to laugh . . . and
  he laughed . . . and he laughed . . . and he laughed.

Tracking a Woozle is more fun with two

'It's a very funny thing,' said Bear, 'but there seem to be *two* animals now. This – whatever it is – has been joined by another – whatever-it-is – and the two of them are now proceeding in company. Would you mind coming with me, Piglet, in case they turn out to be Hostile Animals?' Piglet scratched his ear in a nice sort of way, and said that he had nothing to do until Friday, and would be delighted to come, in case it really *was* a Woozle . . . So off they went together.

Helping someone is a Grand Thing to do

So with these words he unhooked it, and carried it back to Eeyore; and when Christopher Robin had nailed it on in its right place again, Eeyore frisked about the forest, waving his tail so happily that Winnie-the-Pooh came over all funny, and had to hurry home for a little snack of something to sustain him. And, wiping his mouth half an hour afterwards, he sang to himself proudly:

Who found the Tail?
'I,' said Pooh,
'At a quarter to two
(Only it was quarter to eleven really),
I found the Tail!'

It might not be your fault

'Pooh,' said Owl severely, 'did *you* do that?'
'No,' said Pooh humbly. 'I don't *think* so.'
'Then who did?'
'I think it was the wind,' said Piglet. 'I think
your house has blown down.'
'Oh, is that it? I thought it was Pooh.'
'No,' said Pooh.
'If it was the wind,' said Owl, considering the
matter, 'then it wasn't Pooh's fault.
No blame can be attached to him.'

A bad day can
always improve

Eeyore, the old grey Donkey, stood by the side of the stream, and looked at himself in the water. 'Pathetic,' he said. 'That's what it is. Pathetic . . . But nobody minds. Nobody cares. Pathetic, that's what it is.'

There was a crackling noise in the bracken behind him, and out came Pooh . . .

'You seem so sad, Eeyore.'

'Sad? Why should I be sad? It's my birthday. The happiest day of the year.'

'Your birthday?' said Pooh in great surprise . . .

'Stay there!' he called to Eeyore, as he turned and hurried back home as quick as he could; for he felt that he must get poor Eeyore a present of *some* sort at once, and he could always think of a proper one afterwards.

'After all,' said Rabbit to himself, 'Christopher Robin depends on Me. He's fond of Pooh and Piglet and Eeyore, and so am I, but they haven't any Brain. Not to notice. And he respects Owl, because you can't help respecting anybody who can spell TUESDAY, even if he doesn't spell it right; but spelling isn't everything. There are days when spelling Tuesday simply doesn't count. And Kanga is too busy looking after Roo, and Roo is too young and Tigger is too bouncy to be of any help, so there's really nobody but Me, when you come to look at it. I'll go and see if there's anything he wants doing, and then I'll do it for him. It's just the day for doing things.'

Recognise your unique talents

Enjoy being yourself – a Bear can and should

I could spend a happy morning
          Seeing Roo,
I could spend a happy morning
          Being Pooh.
For it doesn't seem to matter,
     If I don't get any fatter
   (And I *don't* get any fatter),
          What I do.

The sun was so delightfully warm, and the stone,
which had been sitting in it for a long time, was so
warm, too, that Pooh had almost decided to go on
being Pooh in the middle of the stream for the rest
of the morning, when he remembered Rabbit.

'What do you like doing best in the world, Pooh?'. . .
he thought that being with Christopher Robin was
a very good thing to do, and having Piglet near
was a very friendly thing to have; and so, when he
had thought it all out, he said, 'What I like best in
the whole world is Me and Piglet going to see You,
and You saying "What about a little something?"
and Me saying, "Well, I shouldn't mind a little
something, should you, Piglet," and it being a
hummy sort of day outside, and birds singing.'
'I like that too,' said Christopher Robin,
'but what I like *doing* best is Nothing.'

Doing Nothing with your friends is the best thing in the world

Sometimes you are wonderful,
even when you don't know it.

'Did I really do all that?' he said at last.
'Well,' said Pooh, 'in poetry – in a piece of
poetry – well, you *did it*, Piglet, because the
poetry says you did. And that's how people know.'
'Oh!' said Piglet. 'Because I – I thought I did
blinch a little. Just at first. And it says,
"Did he blinch no no." That's why.'
'You only blinched inside,' said Pooh, 'and
that's the bravest way for a Very Small Animal
not to blinch that there is.'
Piglet sighed with happiness, and began to
think about himself. He was BRAVE . . .

You can always remedy an Awful Mistake

'Where was I going? Ah, yes, Eeyore.' He got up
slowly. And then, suddenly, he remembered.
He had eaten Eeyore's birthday present!
'*Bother*!' said Pooh. 'What *shall* I do?
I *must* give him *something*.'
For a little while he couldn't think of anything.
Then he thought: 'Well, it's a very nice pot,
even if there's no honey in it, and if I washed
it clean, and got somebody to write "*A Happy
Birthday*" on it, Eeyore could keep things in it,
which might be Useful.'

Even gloomy people cheer up occasionally

But Eeyore wasn't listening. He was taking
the balloon out, and putting it back again,
as happy as could be . . .

No one is perfect

... Owl, wise though he was in many ways, able to read and write and spell his own name WOL ... somehow went all to pieces over delicate words like MEASLES and BUTTEREDTOAST.

PLES CNOKE
IF AN RNSR
IS NOT REQID

Someone will have confidence in you

'And if anyone knows anything about anything,'
said Bear to himself, 'it's Owl who knows
something about something,' he said, 'or my
name's not Winnie-the-Pooh,' he said.
'Which it is,' he added. 'So there you are.'

'A week!' said Pooh gloomily. '*What about meals?*'
'I'm afraid no meals,' said Christopher Robin, 'becau
of getting thin quicker. But we *will* read to you.'
Bear began to sigh, and then found he couldn't
because he was so tightly stuck; and a tear
rolled down his eye, as he said:
'Then would you read a Sustaining Book, such
as would help and comfort a Wedged Bear
in Great Tightness?'

Books can Comfort
and Sustain

Everyone can be useful!

'We'll read to you,' said Rabbit cheerfully.
'And I hope it won't snow,' he added. 'And I say,
old fellow, you're taking up a good deal of room
in my house – *do* you mind if I use your back
legs as a towel-horse? Because, I mean, there
they are – doing nothing – and it would be very
convenient just to hang the towels on them.'

For a week Christopher Robin read that sort of book at the North end of Pooh, and Rabbit hung his washing on the South end . . . and in between Bear felt himself getting slenderer and slenderer. And at the end of the week Christopher Robin said, '*Now*!'

So he took hold of Pooh's front paws and Rabbit took hold of Christopher Robin, and all Rabbit's friends and relations took hold of Rabbit, and they all pulled together . . . And for a long time Pooh only said '*Ow*!' . . . And '*Oh*!' . . . And then, all of a sudden, he said '*Pop*!' just as if a cork were coming out of a bottle. And Christopher Robin and Rabbit and all Rabbit's friends and relations went head-over-heels backwards . . . and on the top of them came Winnie-the-Pooh – free!

It is always possible to get out of a tight place

Try singing to warm
your soul

They were out of the snow now, but it was very cold, and to keep themselves warm they sang Pooh's song right through six times, Piglet doing the tiddely-poms and Pooh doing the rest of it, and both of them thumping on the top of the gate with pieces of stick at the proper places. And in a little while they felt much warmer, and were able to talk again.

Sing Ho! for the life of a Bear!
Sing Ho! for the life of a Bear!
I don't much mind if it rains or snows,
'Cos I've got a lot of honey on my nice new nose!
I don't much care if it snows or thaws,
'Cos I've got a lot of honey on my nice clean paws!
Sing Ho! for a Bear!
Sing Ho! for a Pooh!
And I'll have a little something in an hour or two!

Treat yourself every now and then

Savour every moment

'What do you like doing best in the world, Pooh?'
'Well,' said Pooh, 'what I like best –' and then he
had to stop and think. Because although Eating
Honey *was* a very good thing to do, there was
a moment just before you began to eat it which
was better than when you were, but he
didn't know what it was called.

You are very lovable –
love yourself!

'Oh, Bear!' said Christopher Robin.
'How I do love you!'
'So do I,' said Pooh.

Everyone is different, but equally Important

So after breakfast they went round to see Piglet, and Pooh explained as they went that Piglet was a Very Small Animal who didn't like bouncing, and asked Tigger not to be too Bouncy just at first. And Tigger, who had been hiding behind trees and jumping out on Pooh's shadow when it wasn't looking, said that Tiggers were only bouncy before breakfast, and that as soon as they had had a few haycorns they became Quiet and Refined.

There's always someone who can help

'It's Christopher Robin!' said Piglet.
'*He'll* know what to do.'
They hurried up to him.
'Oh, Christopher Robin,' began Pooh.
'And Eeyore,' said Eeyore.
'Tigger and Roo are right up the Six Pine
Trees, and they can't get down, and –'
'And I was just saying,' put in Piglet, 'that
if only Christopher Robin –'
'*And* Eeyore –'
'If only you were here, then we could
think of something to do.'

There probably isn't a Woozl following you

Christopher Robin came slowly down his tree. 'Silly old Bear,' he said, 'what *were* you doing? First you went round the spinney twice by yourself, and then Piglet ran after you and you went round again together, and then you were just going round a fourth time –'

'Wait a moment,' said Winnie-the-Pooh, holding up his paw.

He sat down and thought, in the most thoughtful way he could think. Then he fitted his paw into one of the Tracks . . . and then he scratched his nose twice, and stood up.

'Yes,' said Winnie-the-Pooh.

'I see now,' said Winnie-the-Pooh.

BANG!!!???***!!!

Piglet lay there, wondering what had happened.
At first he thought that the whole world had
blown up; and then he thought that perhaps only
the Forest part of it had; and then he thought
that perhaps only *he* had, and he was now alone
in the moon or somewhere, and would never
see Christopher Robin or Pooh or Eeyore again.
And then he thought, 'Well, even if I'm in the
moon, I needn't be face downwards all the time,'
so he got cautiously up and looked about him.
He was still in the Forest!
'Well, that's funny,' he thought. 'I wonder what
that bang was. I couldn't have made such a noise
just falling down. And where's my balloon?
And what's that small piece of damp rag doing?'

Things are often better
than they seem

It might never happen!

'Supposing a tree fell down, Pooh,
when we were underneath it?'
'Supposing it didn't,' said Pooh
after careful thought.
Piglet was comforted by this . . .

Eleven o'clock will always cheer you up

He looked up at his clock, which had stopped
at five minutes to eleven some weeks ago.
'Nearly eleven o'clock,' said Pooh happily. 'You're
just in time for a little smackerel of something,'
and he put his head into the cupboard. 'And then
we'll go out, Piglet, and sing my song to Eeyore.'

You're all right, really

'Tigger is all right, *really*,' said Piglet lazily.
'Of course he is,' said Christopher Robin.
'Everybody is *really*,' said Pooh. 'That's what I think,'
said Pooh. 'But I don't suppose I'm right,' he said.
'Of course you are,' said Christopher Robin.

Pooh and his friends will always be there for you

But, of course, it isn't really Good-bye, because
the Forest will always be there . . . and anybody
who is Friendly with Bears can find it.

In that enchanted place on the top of
the Forest a little boy and his Bear
will always be playing.